SECRETS TO RAISING A SMARTER CHILD

DR DHEERAJ MEHROTRA

ISBN 979-8885591564-9

Contents

Preface

Hey Guys!

Congratulations on being a wow parent. Parenting does not just mean raising a child as you were raised, instead taking responsibility for the lives of others in addition to self. The book featuring "Secrets to Raising a Smarter Child" encapsulates measures and strategies to be an excellent parent and deliver the joyful journey with your kids with passion and delight.

A GOOD PARENTING CAUSES HEADACHES, BUT BAD PARENTING CAUSES HEARTACHES

I hope you all enjoy the learning and engage yourselves as great parents!

Dr Dheeraj Mehrotra

CHAPTER ONE

SECRETS TO RAISING A SMARTER CHILD

Secret # 1
Believe in PARENTING Power! Enjoy the blessing you have received as a PARENT. Be proud and stay Fit!

Secret # 2
Get ready for the hardest job: Parenting is the hardest job that you have ever done or will be doing. Get ready to learn the tricks of the trade. Be prepared for different situations.

Secret # 3

Lean "how to do caring for the baby" Parenting begins from pregnancy. Once you are pregnant, you will have to stop smoking and drinking. You have to avoid tea and coffee. You need to eat healthy food, get enough rest and so on.

Secret # 4

Learn from experienced parents: If you are a first-time parent, there is so much to learn from people who have already raised kids. Your parents can teach you so many things.

Secret # 5

Learn to Stop complaining: Your child may not follow you, but this does not mean you should start complaining. When you make complaints, your child's ego will be hurt. A good parent loves their child for who they are not who they will be.

Secret # 6

Keep your expectations high: You should always have high expectations about your child, this will boost confidence in your child. Good parent allows their children to be responsible for their behaviour.

Secret # 7

Encourage your child to take reasonable risks: Risk-taking is good for personal development, you should encourage your child to take reasonable risks. We must treat our kids as our equals and not as subordinates.

Secret # 8

Don't react immediately: When your child makes mistakes, don't react immediately. Analyze the situations thoroughly before, you react. Love your child no matter what. No one is perfect, we have all made mistakes and will continue to.

Secret # 9

Give your children appropriate ways to feel powerful. Let your kid do his own struggle: Struggle is an important mantra to succeed in life, don't make things easier for the child.

Secret # 10
Keep everything real: Don't lie to your child, let him understand how things are in the real world. If your child is testing you through.... A temper tantrum, anger, crying, disrespect.... It is best to leave the room and tell him to talk to him later.

Secret # 11
Listen to your kids: When your kid wants to say something, don't ignore him. Stop what you are doing and actively listen to him. Don't interrupt, express your opinion only after he stops. Be firm YET kind!

Secret # 12
Talk to your child: Don't wait for your child to strike the communication. Ask him questions, encourage him to ask a question.
MOM & DAD: "Do not compare me to other children consistently, it makes me jealous."

Secret # 13
Be communicative: Always find time for communication, never disconnect your kid's

call. Communication helps you understand your child as well as helps him to understand his parent.

Secret # 14

Show Good Judgment: Teach what is right and what is wrong. Make them follow the right things and avoid doing wrongs. Never try to motivate your child by withdrawing your love.

Secret # 15

Stick to Your Rules: When you make a rule, you should stick to these rules. If you don't follow the rules, how can you expect your child to follow the rules? Never give in to pleas, tears, demands or pouting.

Secret # 16

Become a role model: If you want your kid to be good, you should be a good person yourself. The kids are always watching you, never doing anything bad in front of them.

Secret # 17

Control your emotions: If you express extreme

emotions (anger, frustrations etc.) in front of your child, your child is likely to copy that (believe me, children are good at imitating).

Secret # 18
Let them imitate: Human beings learn by imitation, in fact, imitation is the first learning method. Encourage skill development through imitation.

Secret # 19
Show Love: Children are not very good at deciphering the meaning behind words. Therefore, a simple "I love you" does not mean anything to them. Show them your love through hugs, kisses, even gifts.

Secret # 20
Be positive: If you are positive, your child will grow into an optimist individual. You might fail at something, however, don't should your failures.
Mom & Dad: " Simply correct the mistakes I make instead of yelling at me."

Secret # 21

Avoid negativity: If you are a negative person, your child might grow into a pessimistic individual. If you show your positive side, your child will not incorporate negativity.

Secret # 22

Make them feel secure: Your child should understand you as a safe haven. They need to feel secure around you. Let your child feel that he is safe with you.

Secret # 23

Build trust: If you want your child to rely on you, you should build trust. If he shares his secret, don't reveal it to anyone, not even your partner.

Secret # 24

Reflect on your experience: Your childhood experience can help you in your parenting journey. If there were things that you liked, implement those things. If you had a bad experience, avoid those things.

Secret # 25

Share your life experience: There are so many things that the child can learn from you as parents. Tell your kids everything you know, how you did certain things, how you behaved and how you nourished with time.

Secret # 26

Find time for yourself: Don't be too harsh on yourself, becoming a good parent does not mean you don't care about your well being. If you are happy with yourself, you can make your child happy.

Secret # 27

Don't spank: If you spank, your child will learn to become violent.
Mom & Dad: "Encourage me to finish my homework. Don't threaten me. It makes me

dislike studies"

Secret # 28

Read your child: In order to understand your child, you need to understand child psychology. Try to analyze how your child feels and thinks. Respect his opinion too!

Secret # 29

Read books: There is a lot of research in parenting, read books on parenting and try to implement what you have learned. Mom & Dad: "When you show faith in me, it develops a whole lot of courage in me".

Secret # 30

Talk to other parents: Experienced parents will always have something important to tell you. Mom & Dad: "Give me little chores to do and help out at home. It teaches me life skills"

Secret # 31

Let them be: Don't ask your child to be someone, always encourage them to be themselves. Don't tell them to be like his friend Ravi," instead, help them to be Shashank (your

child's name).

Secret # 32
Understand your privilege: The child is a gift of God, understand your privilege as a parent. The child did not arrive at torture you, instead to make you happy.

Secret # 33
Don't make them act like adults: A child grows into an adult. It is a natural process. Let your child remain a child, don't expect them to act like adults. You don't expect an adult to behave like a child, why should you expect your child to act like an adult?

Secret # 34
Teach survival skills: Life is full of surprises; you never know what comes next. Therefore, make your child ready for various circumstances, for instance, teach them what to do when earthquakes come, or when stranger approaches and alike.

Secret # 35

Let them learn: You are certainly more knowledgeable than your child, but your child is not ignorant, he has his own intelligence. Let him learn things in his own ways. The more they learn the more they earn in life.

Secret # 36

Nurture your child's natural spirituality: Let your child grow naturally into his own spiritual understanding, let him learn from his surroundings. Practice Experiential Learning with the kids.

Secret # 37

Don't meddle: Do you like people meddling in your own business? Certainly not. A child has his own world, don't Create an atmosphere of meddling.

Secret # 38

Create a supporting atmosphere: Do you want your child to live in fear? Create an atmosphere where the child can do what he wants. Letting him do whatever he wants does not mean, the child is allowed to commit wrongs all the time.

Secret # 39
Let the child be free: The thinking that you are his parent and you will never harm him has given birth to the thought that you should control your kids. Too much control is bad.

Secret # 40
Give them true love: True love is not connected with showering your child with kisses or giving everything your child wants. True love means, you are doing what is best for him.

Secret # 41
Create a loving atmosphere: If you are harsh on your child, he will never trust you, he might even hate you. Never ever compare your one child with the other. Each child is a creative genius.

Secret # 42
Teach your kids about TAXES!
Eat 30% of their ICE Cream.
Mom & Dad: "When I am throwing a huge tantrum, at times, all I need is a big hug."

Secret # 43

Don't boss around: Don't judge the child from an ivory tower, instead sit below the child and try to understand his mind.

Secret # 44
Make yourself attractive: If you can attract your child, he will like you. When he likes you, he will follow you.

Secret # 45
Give love, take affection: Love is a two-way process, if you want to be loved, you need to give love. Love your child and he will shower with affection.

Secret # 46
Respect your child to be respected: Like love, respect is also a two-way process. If you respect your child, the child will certainly respect you.

Secret# 47
Spend quality time: In order to understand your child, you should spend quality time. If you spend quality time, you will also develop a

friendship bond with your child.

Secret# 48

Manage your stress: Parenting can be very stressful. When you are too much stressed out, you might be a little harsh on the child. Manage your stress, so that you don't spew your frustration on the child.

Secret # 49

Manage your anger: Most of us cannot avoid anger, however, when you are with your child, you need to control your anger. If you cannot stop yourself from slamming the door, your child will learn how to slam the door and when to slam the door.

Secret # 50

Develop a healthy relationship with your partner: A good parent is an individual who also has a good relationship with his/her partner. If you have a healthy relationship with your spouse, your child will grow in a healthy environment.

Secret # 51

Give them autonomy: The child is small, yet he

has a distinct personality and individuality.

Secret # 52
Let them be independent: You are his parent, you want your child to be the best, however, does the child want to do what you want him to do? Encourage the child to become self-reliant.

Secret # 53
Provide them opportunities: Let your child explore his hobbies, interests, and skills by giving them opportunities.

Secret # 54
Provide learning environment: Don' t expect your child to pick up his textbook when you switch the TV on.

Secret # 55
Generate good income: You need money to provide good education, upbringing and pay medical bills.

Secret # 56
Save money: If you actually care about your child, you should start saving money and make plans for the better future.

Secret # 57
Behavioral management: Make punishment the last option. Punishment should be used only when all methods of behavioural management have failed.

Secret # 58
Punish your child, but don't be too harsh: Research on parenting and child psychology tell that sometimes punishment is necessary to discipline the child, enforce rules, and encourage learning.

Secret # 59
Give them nutritious food: The child can be very selective about what they eat, encouraging them to eat healthy food.

Secret # 60

Maintain a healthy lifestyle: Go to bed early, wake up early. Don't hang out late at night, don't spend too much time in parties. How you live actually matters to your child.

Secret # 61
Exercise regularly: Teach your child the importance of exercise and take him to jog or cycling.

Secret # 62
Teach tolerance: we live in a multicultural society, people from various cultures are living among us. Teach your child how to appreciate people from other cultures.

Secret # 63
Teach religion: It is ok to encourage your child to participate in spiritual or religious activities, however, don't force religious guidance. Teach your kids to RESPECT All RELIGIONS.

Secret # 64
Keep an eye: You should be aware of your child's activities in school, in after-school programs, and in community activities.

Secret # 65
Know your child's friends: You should know your child's friends; you should know the parents of your child's friends. Your child's friend can tell you so many things about your child.

Secret # 66
Take precautions to protect your child: Danger is lurking around. Even a simple swing can be dangerous. Watch your child's back.

Secret# 67
Take the helm: Don't let the child dictate you. Once you play by his rules out of love, there will be no turning back. Therefore, let the child know you are in charge.

Secret # 68

Set a boundary: The world can be very confusing for your child, therefore set a boundary so that your child can explore his passion in a safe environment.

Secret # 69
Don't hurt his self-esteem: Your child is a distinct individual, he has his self-esteem. You don't want anyone to hurt your self-respect, do you?

Secret # 70
Don't clip your child's wings: If your child wants to do things like tying the shoelace, wearing the shirt etc. let him do it. This is good for you as well.

Secret# 71
Never try to fix everything. Let your child find his own solution. Don't meddle until he gives up. By giving the child to find his own solutions, you are teaching him self-reliance and resilience.

Secret # 72
Discipline your child: Disciplining the child begins from home. You should make standard

rules on what is allowed and what is not allowed.

Secret # 73

Remember discipline is not about exercising restriction: Your child needs to be disciplined. However, discipline does not mean restricting them. Disciplining means letting them behave properly so that they can become a good person.

Secret # 74

Discourage violence: Children are destructive by nature; they enjoy throwing things, breaking things. You should discourage violence early on.

Secret # 75

Don't make too many rules: Children cannot absorb too many rules. Focus on the things that actually matter such as study time, playtime and dinner time, with Tech-Candy Time on their priority!

Secret # 76

Don't be rude: If you are rude to your children, it is very likely that also become rude to you. If you talk rudely, they will also talk rudely. If you behave rudely, children will also behave rudely.

Secret # 77
Be polite: Children will understand you when you are polite. If you are impolite, they may follow you in the beginning, however, later they will become a rebel.

Secret # 78
Understand the age group: Your child passes through various stages, you should understand these ages and treat accordingly. Parenting a baby is different from parenting a toddler.

Secret # 79
Treat them like a person: Children are also distinct personalities. They want respect, they want to be understood, and they want to be heard.

Secret # 80

Give them choices: You should not force your children to do want you actually want them to do. Give them choices, for instance, let them choose whether to read a story-book, play a video game or even enjoy their cloud presence!

Secret # 81

Spend quality time: Children want your time, they want you to be around, and they want you to participate in their activities. Therefore, you must have time for your children.

Secret # 82

Give them books: Books are the source of knowledge. Encourage children to read books. When they are reading, pick up your book and sit with them reading your book.

Secret # 83

Read aloud to children: You can encourage reading habit by reading aloud to your children. You read a paragraph and ask your child to read. Children love to listen to their parents. Reading together creates a bonding.

Secret # 84

Interact with the child: Interaction is the key to

emotional development. You need to ask a lot of questions and get ready to answer your child's questions.

Secret # 85
Give them interactive toys: Interactive toys can not only entertain children but also help them learn so many things. Things like building blocks will help them learn alphabets and numerals.

Secret # 86
Schedule a play time: Children do not like seriousness, therefore, instead of books, they are likely to watch the cartoon. Schedule a play time. You might tell them they can play the game once they finish the breakfast.

Secret # 87
Let them see things: Seeing is believing. Instead of telling what a tiger is or showing a video of a tiger, take them to the zoo and let them see a real tiger. Practice experiential learning on routine.

Secret # 88
Go for co-parenting: Mother and father both have a responsibility to take care of the child. This is imperative for the emotional well-being of the child. Not just mothers, fathers also should take interest in parenting.

Secret # 89
Daddy time: Generally speaking, dads are most of the time not involved in parenting. Dads don't feed their children, they don't clean their children. Research tells kids that are taken care of by dads to excel in school and develop problem-solving skills.

Secret # 90
Mummy time: In most cases, moms are the ones who are around the children all the time. This might bore the children. Moms should create special activities to engage children.

Secret # 91
Create warm memories: You sure have warm memories from your childhood, don't you? Do you remember when your day read stories to you? Do you remember when your mom and you played a board game?

Secret # 92
Create interesting activities: Boredom grabs children easily. The toy they loved a week ago will no longer interest them. Create interesting activities. A simple thing like bathing a dog can be very interesting to children or even watering the plants!

Secret # 93
Become a great cook: Children are very choosy about what they eat. One of the common problems for mothers is feeding her child. Learn cooking and always try new dishes.

Secret # 94
Let them enter the kitchen: Cooking is a fun activity for children. Your child will enjoy cooking with you. Don' t let them play with a knife or go near the stove, however, you can ask them to beat the egg, sort out vegetables and arrange the table. Why not?

Secret# 95
Go for gardening: Children love to play with mud and water. Take them to the garden and

help them sow the seeds, water the plants and explore nature!

Secret # 96
Bring a pet in your home: Children love animals and birds. Having a dog, a cat, a parrot, even a fish in the home will make your children happy. Children love to interact with living things more than non-living things like a toy cars.

Secret # 97
Admit your mistakes: When you admit your mistakes, your children will learn to apologize when they commit wrongs. Admitting your mistakes in front of your child will not diminish your personality.

Secret # 98
Go for a nature walk: Nature can teach a lot of things to your child. You can tell your child how trees help human beings, how human beings are dependent on the ecosystem and even share the geography around!

Secret # 99
Teach them to care for the environment: Tell your child, how the environment relates to human beings. Teach them not to waste, tell them to reuse things. For example, you can tell him how water is important and why he should not wastewater.

Secret # 100
Encourage social responsibility: Picking trash from the garden might sound boring, however, your child might love this if you make this a game.

Secret # 101
Teach them compassion: Help your child understand the power of compassion. Encourage them to be compassionate towards homeless people, animals and the poor.

Secret # 102
Always tell the truth: What kind of child you will bring up if you don't speak the truth? If you want your child to behave right, you should always speak the truth. By speaking the truth, you will be bringing a morally responsible individual.

Secret # 103
Don't lie to your child: If you continuously lie to your children, your child will stop believing you. If you lie, your child will no more respect you, no more love you. Even the white lies can be very damaging.

Secret # 104
Attend all the PTMs, School Functions, Get Together moments at school without fail. When both MOM and DAD go to school together the kids love it!

Secret # 105
Don't nag with your partner: Children raised in families where partners quarrel, are likely to develop into a weak personality. It is very common to have a disagreement with your partner. If you ever happen to argue, always do it when the children are not around.

Secret # 106
Praise in public and criticize in Private. The same goes for your spouse and the kids! Remember this without fail!

Secret # 107
Respect your partner: In families, where the women have a high opinion about their men and vice versa, the children will also have a high opinion about their dads and moms. When you respect your partner, your child will love his dad and mom more.

Secret # 108
Respect the parenting differences: Your idea of parenting might be different from your partner's parenting idea. You need to support your spouse's parenting method because he/she does not mean any harm to the child.

Secret # 109

Praise your child: When your child does something good, praise him. When you praise them, he will be encouraged to do better. Even when he is not doing well, you have to praise him for attempting it.

Secret # 110

Always give positive feedback: A child needs positive feedback. Telling her that the drawing is crap will make her feel worse. Instead of saying the drawing is bad, you have to say, "If you erase this line and draw another curve here, the drawing will be better."

Secret # 111

Avoid negative feedback: Children are easily discouraged by negative feedback. When you give negative feedback as a child might lose interest in attempting the same thing again. Even if your child comes home with an "E" grade, don't give negative feedback on his face.

Secret # 112

Reward your child: Rewards have a wonderful effect on human psychology, even more on children. Reward your child for his achievement. You can tell him he will have a bicycle if he gets an "A" grade in the next exams.

Secret # 113
Cherish his achievements: Your child comes home with good grades, show your appreciation. Your child wins a trophy in a race, place the trophy alongside with your valuables.

Secret # 114
Watch him perform: If your child is participating in any competition, attend the event. If he makes it, hug him, kiss him. If he does not make it, praise him for participating.

Secret # 115
Make him feel special: Your child is very special to you, however, does your child know this? You have to make your child feel special each time and every time!

Secret # 116
Gossip about your child: It makes more sense when your child finds you saying good things

about him to dad than in front of him.

Secret # 117
Trust Yourself: You know your child better than anyone, always trust your gut. Even if you are thinking that you are wrong, it is very likely that you are right.

Secret # 118
Know when to say YES and when to say NO: Disciplining a child can be very tough, you should know when to say yes and when to say no.

Secret # 119
Say NO when your child is distrustful and intolerant: Don't let your child become disrespectful to you or anyone else. Stop him when he becomes intolerant.

Secret # 120
Build confidence: You can build confidence in your child by praising and rewarding his achievements. You can also build confidence in the child by participating in his activities.

Secret # 121
Let him channelize emotions: If your child is angry, divert his mind by asking him to participate in interesting activities. If your child is crying, make him feel secure by hugging tight.

Secret # 122
Teach your kids
EMPATHY by telling them stories of your age/ life with moral lessons.

Secret # 123
Empower yourself with the power of TECHNOLOGY to match the requirements of the KIDS at home!

Secret # 124
Teach ethics: Teach your child what is ethical and what is unethical. Help him understand the difference between ethical and unethical.

Secret # 125

Teach morality: Morality is a distinction between good and evil, morality refers to the right conduct. By teaching morality, try to raise a morally responsible individual.

Secret # 126
Tell them the importance of values: Explain to your child why being good actually matters, how truthfulness will help in life.

Secret # 127
Don' t fight when your child does not eat: Food fight is very common. If your child does not eat a certain food, offer him another dish or ask him what he wants to eat. If he does not want to eat, let it be. Your child will not starve.

Secret # 128
Make a parenting schedule: parenting is a hard work; it can exhaust you thoroughly. Making a schedule can ease your work. Set a timetable for various responsibilities.

Secret # 129
Encourage your kids to do creative things: Ask

your child to sing, dance, write, draw, play instruments. Creative activities like these will boost his mental capacity.

Secret # 130
Encourage physical activities: Research shows that brain development is connected with physical activity. Encourage your children to walk, run, play outdoor games.

Secret # 131
Take your child to regular medical checkups: You should get all the required vaccines for your child. You also need to take your child to the doctor regularly. Never ignore the health-related complaints.

Secret # 132
Take care of personal hygiene: Encourage your child to brush teeth, wash his hands and feet, take bath regularly. Learning should be made a habit rather than an occasional occurrence.

Secret # 133
Be vigilant about safety: Always make sure that the babies and toddlers are not left alone. Tell him to wear a helmet when he is riding his bike

or scooter.

Secret # 134
**Think twice before administering drugs:
Antibiotics can cause problems, therefore,
always look for the alternatives.**

Secret # 135
**Promote independence: Your child's
development will be hindered if he is too much
depended on you. You need to tell him that you
are always with him, yet make him go alone.**

Secret # 136
**Never push too far: Have high expectation.
Expect your child to do great things, tell him to
aim high, however, never push him too far.**

Secret # 137
Let your child try: Resist in doing what your child can do herself. Your child might take 30 minutes to eat his meal by himself and if you spoon feed, you may do it in 10 minutes, however, by not letting your child do on his own, you are hindering his learning process.

Secret # 138
Don't redo what your child has already done: Unless it is very necessary, don't fix what your child has already done. This will discourage your child to do it on her own.

Secret # 139
Let them solve the problems: What do you do when you see your child trying to get a toy from the shelf that she is finding hard to reach? If you want to get it for her, just stop.

Secret # 140
Give your child assignment: Encourage your child to do things like sorting out the coloured dresses for the laundry, picking books from the floor, picking the trash from the garden.

Secret # 141
Develop a routine: Make a routine for your child to read books, do his assignments, play games and watch TV. Give him or her a say in your daily routine.

Secret # 142
Develop predictable routines: When the children follow the same routine every day, they learn quickly. The routine should include things like brushing teeth before going to bed, washing hands before eating and offering prayers at least once a day.

Secret # 143
Encourage cooperation: Make your child understand that human beings are social animals and cooperation is the key to become successful. Teach cooperation by asking your child to get along with his peers.

Secret # 144
Teach manners: Children are deft in throwing tantrums. One of the ways to control tantrums is by teaching them manners. You have to teach them how to behave well.

Secret # 145

Make rules: You need to make rules and make your child strictly follow these rules. The rules for the children can be as simple as "do not litter around" or as complex as "do not talk to the strangers."

Secret # 146

Be funny and humorous: Sometimes you are required to make faces to make your child laugh, sometimes you are required to dress funnily to make your child smile.

Secret # 147

Teach time management: You should teach your child when to stop watching TV, when to stop playing a video game and when to go to bed.

Secret # 148

Use infographics and images to teach your child: Research tells that children learn faster if infographics and images are used. Give them picture books to help them understand things.

Secret # 149
Let them watch instructional and educational videos: Children learn faster when they watch instructional and educational videos.

Secret # 150
Use child-friendly language: Tell your child "If you finish your homework, we might go to the park." Or, "Finish your homework, we'll go to the park." You can see the difference in reactions.

Secret # 151
Don' t use vulgar words: Never use curse words, vulgar words in front of the child. No "shit" no "IDIOT". Make them aware about the signs of CHILD ABUSE too!

Secret # 152
Don' t compare your child with another child: When you begin to compare your child with another child, jealousy and enmity will develop.

Secret # 153

Have a movie time: Everyone needs entertainment? Take your child to the movie, or have a movie time in the home.

Secret # 154
Play music: Music will not only unburden your exhausted mind but also make your child happy.

Secret # 155
Encourage teamwork: What if children are fighting over the same toy? You can tell one child to play for 10 minutes and then give it to another to play for 10 minutes.

Secret # 156
Let your child settle his own dispute: If the children are debating, don't interfere unless one of them goes violent. Let the children settle their own disputes.

Secret # 157
Learn how to divert your child's mind. If your child is drawing on the wall, bring chart paper and ask him to draw on the paper.

Secret # 158
Learn to manage good-bye meltdowns: Your child may not want to leave you and go to school. Give him something like your picture, a heart-shaped tissue to make him feel that you are with him.

Secret # 159
Help them in righting their wrongs: When your child tears papers and throw them over the floor, ask him to collect the pieces and throw them in the dustbin. Make " Sorry" and "Thank you" their favourite language.

Secret # 160
Reprimand immediately: If your child does something wrong, reprimand immediately. Don't wait until you get home.

Secret # 161
Make sure they get enough sleep: Children are

very proactive, they need rest. Research says if a sixth grader child loses one hour of sleep, his intelligence will be reduced to that of a fourth-grader.

Secret # 162
Raise honest kids: Honesty is the best policy is an old saying. However, research has proved that when the child is honest, he will grow up into a responsible human being. Your child might lie in order to please you or get benefits. Always check whether the child is telling truth or not.

Secret # 163
You need rules: Kids need rules, so do you. Setting rules for kids also mean you have your own rules to follow. If you don't want your kid to watch TV late at night, you also need to avoid watching TV late at night.

Secret # 164
Too much control is bad: The kids whose parents are too strict are the ones who do drugs, drink and smoke. Never do so in front of them ever too!

Secret # 165

Don't let boredom get into your child: If you are too busy for your child, your child might be bored. When a child is bored, he will try to take refuge in activities such as smoking, drinking, and drugs.

Secret # 166

Get into healthy arguments: Research has shown that moderate argument has a positive effect on children.

Secret # 167

Teach them to be grateful: Being grateful is great quality. Your children must learn how to express gratitude.

Secret # 168

Create the right atmosphere: You need to have a child-friendly environment in your house. Creating the right atmosphere is a big part of parenthood. The right atmosphere implies happiness, love, compassion, and discipline.

Secret # 169
Don't impose your dream: You might have wanted to become a doctor but ended by being a salesperson. Don't put pressure on your child to fulfil your dream.

Secret # 170
Know what the child needs: You have a business and you see your child as your successor. This is quite reasonable. However, does your child want to follow in your footsteps?

Secret # 171
Don't pamper: It is true that you need to make your child feel special. However, if you are too much bragging about your child, you are spoiling him.

Secret # 172
Be ready to learn from your child: As a parent, you are the first teacher for your child. However, there are so many things that your child can teach you. Having a child means you are ready to learn so many things.

Secret # 173
Be joyful: Nobody forced you to become a parent, it was your own choice. If you are showing tension, anger, fear, anxiety, and jealousy every now and then, what will the child learn?

Secret # 174
Improving behavioural problems in children: Toddlers show tantrums, teens are rebellious by nature. You cannot solve the behavioural problems in children until you understand their minds and know what exactly they want. Communicate as much as you can to sort out the problems.

Secret # 175
Learn how to entertain the children: If you can keep the children busy, you will win the battle to keep them quiet. There are various ways to entertain your child, find out what's your child's favourite.

Secret # 176
Go for outings: Like you, children also get bored with routine life, then them to outings to

make life interesting. This will also create a
deep bonding.

Secret # 177

Organize children parties: In order to show
how much you love him, you need to organize
children parties and invite your child's friends.
Parties are good for the children as well as
parents as they encourage social interactions
amongst the parents.

Secret # 178

Check the development process: Make sure
you are aware of the changes in your children
bodies. Guide them about the changes in their
personality, character and impart them about
SEX EDUCATION before they learn from the
outside world.

Secret # 179

Check the learning process: Find out how your
child is learning. Look into his notebooks,
school reports and homework. Never guide
them to their homework directly. Have an eye
to their study routine.

Secret # 180

Find out if someone is bullying your child: Bullying can be detrimental to mental development. Find out whether your child is being bullied in the neighbourhood or school.

Secret # 181

Find out whether your child is struggling with cyberbullying: It is very common to see children as young as 5 years use the internet. Check for the signs of cyberbullying.

Secret # 182

Check your children's online activities: The Internet is a source of information and knowledge. However, there are also many bad things over the internet. Be aware of their user IDs' and Passwords. A Good Parent is a Friend of their kids on Social Networking Sites.

Secret # 183

Exercise parental control on cable TV: TV is a good source of learning and entertainment. However, TV also brings channels that can harm the child.

Secret # 184

Exercise parental control on the internet: In order to stop children from checking porn sites and other illegal sites, you need to block malicious sites.

Secret # 185

Don' t' let them choose friends over parents: When it comes to confiding something, children will always go to their friends. However, their friends are not the best people to give them advice. You can be your childhood friends and encourage them to confide in you.

Secret # 186

Let them choose their own career: You know what is best for your children. However, what you think is the best might not be the best for them. Advise them, but let them take their own path.

Secret # 187
Make yourself available: When your children need you, you must always be available. One mistake can damage their entire life. Respect your parents before your KIDS.

Secret # 188
Don' t make them feel they can have it all: Don' t make things easier for your kid. They need to understand things are also not easier for parents.

Secret # 189
Teach the value of money: Money has a great importance in life. Teach your children it is not easy to make money. If you are giving pocket money, check how they are spending.

Secret # 190
Teach them to spend less, save more: If they learn how hard it is to make money, they will learn the importance of spending less and saving more.

Secret # 191
Happy families don' t happen by accident.

They are born from intentional parenting.
Make sure you as a parent value the family
meal and car rides.

Secret # 192
Learn to move on: One day your child becomes
a teen and is ready to leave the house (for
work, education etc.). Your child is your child,
whether he is one month old or 50 years old.

Secret # 193
Don't compromise your own wellbeing: Your
children are your blood and bones, however,
you should never compromise your wellbeing.
Taking care of children does not mean you
have to forget about yourself.

Secret # 194
You don't own your children: One of the main
issues of conflict between the parents and
children is because of the sense of ownership
in parents. Parents tend to think their children
like their pets. Give them freedom of LIVING.

Secret # 195

Get support from others: There is no five-point guide to parenting. Everyone has his/her own parenting style. If you are having difficulty, you can join a parents group and ask for help.

Secret # 196
Raise a giver: There is so much pleasure in giving. Teach your child to become a giver. Let your child understand the importance of giving. Remember YOU just can not raise as you were raised!

Secret # 197
Don't let them get away with meanness: Children can be very mean. They are likely to do emotional blackmailing. Be involved in their lives.

Secret # 198
Ask your kids to help you: When you need extra hands for household work, ask your children to volunteer. This will make your children respond to the family needs. Frequently ask them to do Car Wash or water the plants together.

Secret # 199
Don't yell: Generally speaking, yelling will produce a parent-deaf kid. This shall also cause a dislike with either of the parents by the kid for life.

Secret # 200
Move close, but give them privacy: You need to be close to your kids, but you also should give them privacy. Know their friends and observe their routine. Never bridge their interest but feed their likes.

CHAPTER TWO

PARENTING- THE SKILLFUL PERCEPTION

Friends, for sure, Parenting is an encouraging process that prepares our children for independence. As our child blossoms, there are many things and times when we can help our children dwell with the notion in particular. The inception is towards learning more about your child's development, positive parenting, safety, and health at each stage of your child's life.

As parents, we look forward to the suggestion of being an excellent parent. It transforms toward being constantly straight and explorative to drive changes among our wards.

This will undoubtedly show your youngster exactly how they need to respond in comparable scenarios. If you're easy hostile, your youngster could react to troubles in an easy hostile method that will not profit them. In addition, being a parent, one has to house the page of learning to learn. The practice of good parenting is modelled through an orientation of actions and interactions that you as parents have with your child. Hence, it is driven with purpose and end goals in mind to nurture the tiny tots or the teenagers in functional.

Well, with the dwelling of parenting skills on the page, when the kid does glitch, ensure that you constantly slam the actions and not the youngster. Do not inform them that they misbehaved for doing something. Instead, describe why what they did was incorrect, and afterwards describe what they ought to have done instead. Attempt to express your description in favourable terms. Above all, Parenting is both a satisfying and challenging facet of life. The ideas that comply with are made to reduce the obstacles and enhance the benefits. By following up with them, you are particular to boost your parenting abilities and develop a much better partnership with your youngsters.

Also, keep in pace and mind, if you have greater than one youngster, you must pay the same quantity of focus to every one of them, whatever their ages are. You do not desire one kid to be disregarded-- this can create them to reveal animosity towards you when they grow older. This activates a strong bond of liking, caring and concern at all times.

An excellent parenting suggestion is to provide your kids with personal privacy in some cases. If you're constantly paranoid concerning what they're doing or that they're socialising with, you can shed a great deal of your youngsters' trust fund. Find out to withdraw every so often and allow your youngsters to have some personal privacy.

A crucial idea regarding parenting is to make sure that you establish time apart to play. This is important because kids utilise playtime to discover and create their abilities. When you play, you can conveniently show them lessons and attach to them in manners ins which are unattainable.

Offer your youngster options whenever you can. This can aid to stay clear of the never finishing fight of attempting to obtain your kid to make the one point you desire. A kid is receptive to options, also at a young age. It allows them to feel a feeling of control as well as success.

Make sure to take a while far from your kids. This benefits you, however, additionally for them. It enables you to have some grownup time yet likewise educates your kids exactly how to be much more independent. If you are most likely to leave for more fabulous than an hour, makes sure they recognise when you will certainly return.

Whether you are a collection of moms and dads residing in the same house or different residences, you are most likely to require collaborating as a group regarding every little thing concerning your kid. Discover to differ civilly and discover means to settle any distinctions silently as well as in the most effective passion of your kid.

Source: Internet

CHAPTER THREE

THE IMAGINATIVE PARENTING

When your youngster does glitch, ensure that you constantly slam the actions and not the youngster. Do not inform them that they misbehaved for doing something. Instead, discuss why what they did was incorrect, and after that, discuss what they ought to have done instead. Attempt to express your description in favourable terms. Whether you are a collection of moms and dads residing in the very same residence or different houses, you are most likely to require to collaborate as a group when it pertains to every little thing regarding your kid. Discover to differ civilly, and discover methods to deal with any distinctions silently and in the very best passion of your kid.

Make sure to spend some time far from your youngsters. This benefits you, however, additionally for them. It permits you to have some grown-up time; however, it likewise educates your youngsters just how to be more independent. If you are most likely to leave for greater than an hour, make sure they understand when you return.

A fantastic parenting idea is to offer your youngsters some personal privacy occasionally. If you're constantly paranoid regarding what they're doing or that they're associating, you can shed a great deal of your youngster's dependence on them. Find out to withdraw once in a while and also allow your kids have some personal privacy.

If you have greater than one kid, you must pay the very same quantity of interest to every one of them, whatever their ages are. You do not desire one kid to be disregarded-- this can create them to reveal animosity towards you when they grow older.

A crucial pointer to think about regarding parenting is to ensure that you establish time apart to play. This is critical since kids make use of playtime to discover as well as create their abilities. When you play, you can quickly educate them lessons and link to them in manners ins that are unattainable. Offer your kid selections whenever you can. This can aid to prevent the never finishing fight of attempting to obtain your kid to make the one point you desire. A kid is receptive to selections, also at a young age. It allows them to feel a feeling of control and also achievement. An excellent parenting pointer is to be straight yet tranquil whenever you constantly have trouble. This will undoubtedly show your youngster exactly how they must respond in comparable scenarios. If you're easy hostile, your youngster could react to situations in an easy hostile means which will not profit them. Parenting is both a tough as well as a gratifying facet of life. The pointers that comply with are made to lessen the difficulties and boost the benefits. By following up with them, you are particular to raise your parenting abilities and develop a much better partnership with your youngsters. As parents, we ponder and look forward to better opportunities towards parenting at all times through creating far better parenting abilities and aiding you in having the partnership with your kids that you want. You have made the critical option to *focus on the connection between you and your kids. This selection will undoubtedly settle for several years ahead.*

School & Parents Bonding

Quality School Management requires the expertise of TQM with the reflection of Total Quality Management in Education ignited through the philosophy of KAIZEN, The Scenario:

Parenting in schools explore with a sense of making the device flow with time and pride. The parents, the ultimate customers, deliver with pride as stakeholders in the learning scenario. The need for learning has to encapsulate with the satisfaction of being a child of the new age in certain liberation of making the teaching go gaga in the classrooms in particular. The new-age learning and preface have to make pace with the scenario of delivering the piece of spectrum to make hay within the classrooms to provide and make the same matter the most.

The new definition has to deliver the modern learning format in due concern and spectrum to deviate the perfection. The delivery has to pace with a time of the new age learning defining the structure in the classrooms of an interdisciplinary approach to deliver and walk with the march of time and tide in conjunction with the delivery of pace and formulation in regard. Keeping the pace in view, the new age defines the perforated confluence of all school heads to deal with parents from different backgrounds with different demands.

Momentum within Schools:

The most important thing the Principals or the school leaders do is the exponential equation of multiplying the impact on their wards via the connection with their stakeholders, particularly the Parents for the say. It manipulates the spectrum delivering the proliferation of leadership throughout the organisation, which drives the improved performance in perception to work in the direction to the delivery of making sense go wonders in making the delivery happen to repute and conjunction in particular. The delivery is made to bark on the exact procedure which governs the preface of making the delivery having with the classroom activities and other connect via the school diary of the wards, which delivers to preface to accomplish the task of making the expected deliveries in happening. The prime objectives of the schools need to explore the learning which grows the learners and difference makers and not just the followers. This is on priority to deliver the caring approach to the parent's needs leading to the social system of new-age expectations. The demand of the new age fertilises to the fact of Building, Initiation, discovering and connecting the ideas into making the work demand and desire the exploring of the showcase in fragrance to manipulate and explore the device in designing the replication in the best of order and explores. This scenario fragrance speculates the sense of periodic learning exponentially.

This manipulates the power to explore the identification and prepare and explore the probable expectations of narration in the classrooms. The delivery of the trio, the Parents, Teachers and the Students organises the spectrum of delivery to perform as per the expectations. The friendship delivers in conjunction with the speculation that being friendly with the parents contributes a lot to accomplish. The new age requirement provides inertia of Skills and Attitude, Coaching giving the output as results and the potential as an attribute. Above all, we need to preface the fact giving the framework of "Teaching kids to count is fine, but teaching them what counts is best", shared rightly by Bob Talbert, incorporates the learning mantra in schools with full of wisdom and pride in particular.

Learning in schools has had a new dimension of demands with the perfection of the fact to share:

"I didn't just grow up. I was taught to speak when I entered a room. Say please and thank you, have respect for my elders, set up off my lazy butt, and let the elder in the room have my

chair. Say 'yes sir' and 'no sir', lend a helping hand to those in need. Hold the door for the person behind me, say 'excuse me' when needed, and love people for who they are and not for what I can get from them. I was also taught to treat people how I wanted to be treated. "

The share I received via my WhatsApp community, without identifying the source, I explored my learning in a big soothing way and shared the same to the perfection of making the job done and studying in a way. As a matter of fact, with sharing,

As about modern age learning:

A child can teach us three things:

a.

To be happy for no reason.

b.

To always be curious

c.

To fight tirelessly for something.

We can devise the same spectrum for our partnership with the Parents to look for the dimensions that draft the new fragrance folly to make the cult explore. This series prefers to make the spectrum make and deliver the share in conjunction. The show makes to perform the scope to provide the means in the best possible manner.

Cheers to the education leaders for making the Learning Exciting via connectivity with Parents, Teachers and Students!

About The Author

Dheeraj Mehrotra, MS, MPhil, PhD (Education Management) honoris causa., a white and a yellow belt in SIX SIGMA, a Certified NLP Business Diploma holder, is an Educational Innovator, Author, with expertise in Six Sigma In Education, Academic Audits, Neuro-Linguistic Programming (NLP), Total Quality Management In Education, an Experiential Educator, a CBSE Resource towards School Assessment (SQAA), CCE, JIT, Five S, and KAIZEN. He has authored over 40 books on Computer Science for ICSE/ ISC/ CBSE Students, over 60 books of academic interest for education excellence, and Six Sigma. A former Principal at De Indian Public School, New Delhi, (INDIA) with an ample teaching experience of over Two Decades, he is a certified Trainer for Quality Circles/ TQM in Education and QCI Standards for School Accreditation/ Six Sigma in Education. He has also been honoured with the President of India's National Teacher Award in the year 2006 and the Best Science Teacher State Award (By the Ministry of Science and Technology, State of UP), Innovation in Education for his inception of Six Sigma In Education by Education Watch, New Delhi and Education World- Best Teacher Award, BOLT Learner Teacher Award by Air India, 'Innovation in Education Award 2016' by Higher Education Forum (HEF), Gujarat Chapter, among others. He has developed over 150 FREE EDUCATIONAL MOBILE Apps for the Google Play Store exclusively for Teachers, Students, and Parents. This work has been recognised by the LIMCA BOOK OF RECORDS & INDIA BOOK OF RECORDS as the only Indian to draw that feast. Dr Mehrotra is presently working as a PRINCIPAL at

KUNWARS GLOBAL SCHOOL, Lucknow, in India. He has conducted over 1000 workshops globally on "Excellence In Education" integrated with Total Quality Management and Six Sigma, Technology Integration in Education (TIE), Developing towards being ROCKSTAR TEACHERS, including Cyberspace, Cyber Security, Classroom Management, School Leadership & Management, and Innovative teaching within classrooms via Mind Maps, NLP and Experiential Learning in Academics. He is an active TEDx speaker and can be viewed on the youtube TEDx channel. As a premium UDEMY Instructor, he has also developed over 450 courses and is catering to over 8 Lakh students from 180 plus countries.

He can be visited at www.authordheerajmehrotra.com

Books By The Same Author

www.ingramcontent.com/pod-product-compliance
Lightning Source LLC
Chambersburg PA
CBHW031414160726
47993CB00003B/1221